curious about
HAMSTERS

BY M. K. OSBORNE

AMICUS • AMICUS INK

What are you

curious about?

Curious About is published
by Amicus and Amicus Ink
P.O. Box 227
Mankato, MN 56002
www.amicuspublishing.us

Editor: Alissa Thielges
Series Designer: Kathleen Petelinsek
Book Designer: Ciara Beitlich
Photo researcher: Bridget Prehn

Library of Congress Cataloging-in-Publication Data
Names: Osborne, M. K., author.
Title: Curious about hamsters / by M. K. Osborne
Description: Mankato, MN : Amicus, [2021] | Series:
Curious about pets | Includes bibliographical references and
Index. | Audience: Ages 6–9 | Audience: Grades 2–3
Identifiers: LCCN 2019053789 (print) | LCCN 2019053790
(ebook) | ISBN 9781681519678 (library binding) | ISBN
9781681526140 (paperback) | ISBN 9781645490524 (pdf)
Subjects: LCSH: Hamsters as pets—Juvenile literature.
Classification: LCC SF459.H3 K58 2021 (print) | LCC
SF459.H3 (ebook) | DDC 636.935/6—dc23
LC record available at https://lccn.loc.gov/2019053789
LC ebook record available at https://lccn.loc.gov/2019053790

Photos © iStock/Kerrick cover, 1; Shutterstock/Ilyashenko Oleksiy
2, 6; Shutterstock/Lepas 2, 8; iStock/Olena Kurashova 3, 19;
Alamy/Juniors Bildarchiv 5, 15; iStock/Fourleaflover 5 (map);
iStock/onetouchspark 7 (Syrian); Shutterstock/Vishnevskiy Vasily
7 (dwarf), photovova 7 (Siberian), Emilia Stasiak 7 (Roborovski),
Allocricetulus 7 (Chinese); iStock/raw 9; Shutterstock/Perutskyi
Petro 10–11; Shutterstock/WindOfHope 12–13; Shutterstock/
Michaela Vondruska 14; Dreamstime/Oleksandr Lytvynenko
16–17; iStock/Shantell 17; Shutterstock/bergamont 19 (bananas),
UV70 19 (cabbage, broccoli, strawberries), George Dolgikh
19 (spinach), Olga Popova 19 (carrots, celery); Dreamstime/
Fotogigi85 20; Shutterstock/Lena_Graphic Artist 21

Printed in the United States of America

CHAPTER THREE

**Playing with
Your Hamster**

PAGE
16

CHAPTER ONE

Where do hamsters come from?

Wild hamsters live in Asia and Europe. They are shy. Few people see them. In 1930, a scientist was curious about them. He caught 12 of them for research. Some became pets. Today, you can buy a hamster at a pet store.

Born to be wild!
Black-bellied hamsters
live in Europe.

WHERE CAN WILD HAMSTERS BE FOUND?

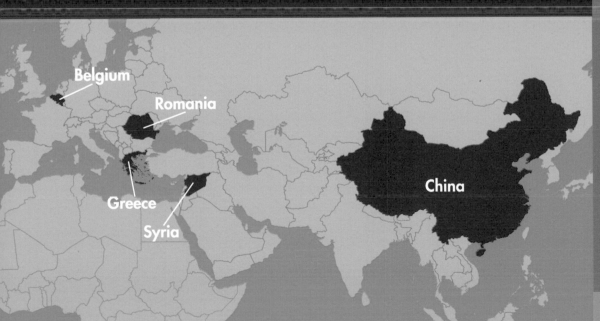

Belgium

Romania

Greece

Syria

China

How long do hamsters live?

Peek-a-boo!

Most hamsters live about two years. It depends on the **breed** of hamster. Syrians are the most common hamsters. They live about two years. Dwarf hamsters are small. Some live up to three years.

SYRIAN

2–2.5 YEARS

DWARF CAMPBELL RUSSIAN

2 YEARS

SIBERIAN

1.5–2 YEARS

ROBOROVSKI DWARF

3–3.5 YEARS

CHINESE

1.5–2 YEARS

AVERAGE LIFE SPANS OF HAMSTER BREEDS

Why does my hamster chew on everything?

Nom nom nom.

Hamsters are **rodents**. Their front teeth never stop growing. To stay healthy, hamsters **gnaw** on things. This wears down the enamel, the outer part of a tooth. It is orange for hamsters. Gnawing keeps the teeth from getting too long.

DID YOU KNOW?
Hamsters don't need baths. They are good at grooming themselves.

Why do hamsters like to run on a wheel?

DID YOU KNOW?
A hamster can run 6 miles (9.7 km) a night on a wheel.

In the wild, hamsters can run for miles. That isn't easy to do in a cage. But your hamster still needs to run. A wheel helps him do this. It keeps him happy and healthy. Then your little buddy won't get too chubby!

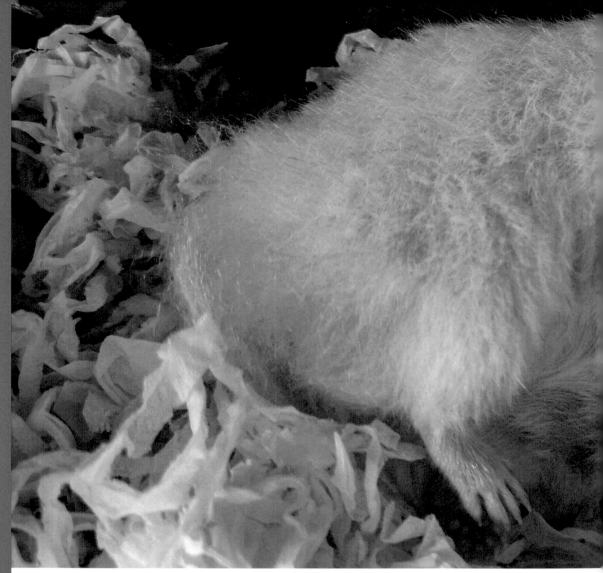

Why is my hamster up at night?

A hamster goes to bed at the same time you wake up for school.

Hamsters are **nocturnal**. They sleep mostly during the day. In the evening, they wake up. This is the best time to play. A sleeping hamster should be left alone. It may bite if woken up suddenly.

Why do hamsters stuff their cheeks with food?

Look at those chubby cheeks! Watching a hamster eat is fun. Hamsters have a **pouch** in each cheek to hold food. You'd be surprised how much a hamster can pack away. The food is taken back to their bed and stored. It will be a snack for later.

Wild hamsters save food to eat in safety. Pet hamsters do this, too.

Can I play with my hamster?

Of course! Most hamsters love games. Playing is a good way to **bond**. Just make sure your pet can't run away or get lost. Try building a cardboard maze. Make it easy at first. Then change it up. Get creative! A paper roll could be a tunnel.

Hamster toys don't have to cost a lot of money.

Can my hamster learn tricks?

Yes. It won't be the same as teaching a dog. But hamsters are smart. Start with an easy trick. To teach a hamster to spin, move a treat in a circle. As your hamster follows the treat, say "Spin."

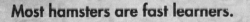

Most hamsters are fast learners.

SAFE HAMSTER TREATS

Bananas

Strawberries

Cabbage

Broccoli

Spinach

Carrots

Celery

A hamster may
think a finger is food.

Ouch! My hamster bit me. What's wrong?

Be gentle when holding your hamster.

Is your hamster young? It may not be **tame** yet. It isn't used to being held or petted. Did you startle it? Hamsters can't see well. A sudden hand coming at them is scary. A finger poking in a cage might look like a treat. To avoid bites, let your hamster come to you.

ASK MORE QUESTIONS

I want a pet hamster. What do I need?

What are wild hamsters like?

Try a BIG QUESTION: Is a hamster a good pet for me?

SEARCH FOR ANSWERS

Search the library catalog or the Internet.
A librarian, teacher, or parent can help you.

Using Keywords
Find the looking glass.

Keywords are the most important words in your question.

If you want to know about:

• what you need to care for a hamster, type: HAMSTER CARE

• what wild hamsters are like, type: WILD HAMSTER BEHAVIOR

FIND GOOD SOURCES

Here are some good, safe sources you can use in your research.
An adult can help you find more.

Books

Is a Hamster a Good Pet for Me?
by Jason Brainard, 2020.

Hamsters: Questions and Answers
by Christina Gardeski, 2017.

Internet Sites

Animal Planet | Pets 101: Hamsters
https://www.animalplanet.com/tv-shows/pets-101/videos/hamster
Animal Planet has educational TV shows about animals.

National Geographic Kids | Hamsters
https://kids.nationalgeographic.com/explore/nature/wild-hamsters/
National Geographic explores the planet. It is a good source for animals and nature.

Every effort has been made to ensure that these websites are appropriate for children. However, because of the nature of the Internet, it is impossible to guarantee that these sites will remain active indefinitely or that their contents will not be altered.

SHARE AND TAKE ACTION

Volunteer at an animal shelter.
Help clean cages and play with hamsters!

Offer to pet sit for a neighbor.

Teach friends and family about hamsters.
Know when it is okay to hold or play with a hamster.

GLOSSARY

bond A close friendship or connection with someone.

breed A group of animals developed from a common ancestor that are similar in looks and behavior.

gnaw To keep biting on something.

nocturnal Active at night.

rodent A mammal with large, sharp front teeth that never stop growing.

tame Gentle and not afraid around people; not wild.

INDEX

About the Author

M. K. Osborne is a children's writer and editor who lives in Minnesota. As an animal lover, Osborne enjoyed researching and writing about pet behavior and communication and hopes to inspire kids to pursue their own inquiries about pets.